jenedypaige

Coming Full Circle

When God Puts the Pieces Together

Jenedy Paige

---── INTRODUCTION ───---

The art in this book was inspired by the death of my son, but I hope the principles in it will help those struggling with any kind of loss. Sometimes we experience the loss of a childhood, or a happy marriage, or the future we anticipated. Trials come in every size and magnitude, but what we are asked to do is the same. We have to sacrifice our broken hearts and go forward in faith. As we turn to God, I know that He is capable of taking every hardship and turning it to our benefit. I hope the images and the words that accompany them will spark a hope in your heart, that you too can rise up after your falls.

"... Suffer the lit
such is t

"Close but Separate"

A few years ago, I was stunned to learn that a friend of mine had lost her 5 year old boy while on a family vacation. My heart immediately broke, that pit in my stomach returned, and a flood of emotions came rushing back in as I contemplated all that my friend would now be going through. A journey all too similar to my own lay before her, and all I could do was cry for her, over and over again.

We met for lunch, and I told her, "I'm not going to even ask how you're doing, because I already know." Tears came to her eyes as she said, "You know... I just miss him. I know he's going to be okay, I know I'm going to see him again, but I just miss him." We commiserated and cried together as we shared stories, finding it difficult to eat the food before us. As we parted ways that afternoon, that phrase, "I just miss him," stayed with me.

It's been years since my little boy passed to the other side of the veil, that beautiful partition between Heaven and Earth, and you know, I just miss him. Years and I still just long to hold him. I know that his spirit is alive and well, every now and then I get a taste of his powerful spirit, but it's only a glimpse. I know he's close to our family and that he's aware of us, but we are still so separate. Gravity holds me here while he is now boundless. Time keeps passing for me, while he has moved to eternity.

I know the separation is important. I know the veil maintains the test that is mortality. As the scholar Neil A. Maxwell so beautifully said, "Without the veil, our brief mortal walk in a darkening world would lose its meaning—for one would scarcely carry the flashlight of faith at noonday and in the presence of the Light of the World" (Patience, 1979). But sometimes the longing of a mother for her child is so deep, you just wish you could reach across if only for a moment.

"I know I'm still a work in progress, and I've got a lot left to do here on earth. I'm thankful for the three other amazing children I get to raise. I'm grateful to have art as a means to process all these difficult emotions. I'm thankful for the knowledge of a loving, wise, Father in Heaven, who has so carefully selected a particular course for me. I know "all things work together for good to them that love God" (Romans 8:28) and that in the end I will only see His wisdom and mercy. But for now..."

I just miss him.

ildren to come unto me, and forbid them not: for of
ngdom of God... And he took them up in his arms..."

Mark 10:14, 16

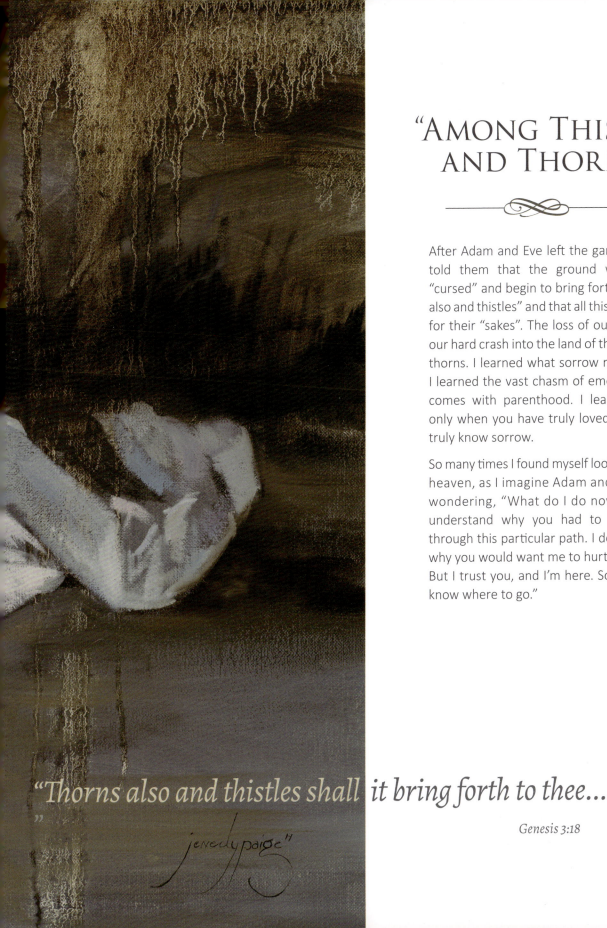

"AMONG THISTLE AND THORN"

After Adam and Eve left the garden, God told them that the ground would be "cursed" and begin to bring forth "thorns also and thistles" and that all this would be for their "sakes". The loss of our son was our hard crash into the land of thistles and thorns. I learned what sorrow really was. I learned the vast chasm of emotion that comes with parenthood. I learned that only when you have truly loved, can you truly know sorrow.

So many times I found myself looking up to heaven, as I imagine Adam and Eve did, wondering, "What do I do now? I don't understand why you had to send me through this particular path. I don't know why you would want me to hurt so much. But I trust you, and I'm here. So help me know where to go."

"Thorns also and thistles shall it bring forth to thee..."

Genesis 3:18

"Stone of Help"

"Come Thou Fount of Every Blessing has long been one of my favorite hymns. I would sing the lyrics, "Here I raise my Ebenezer" having no idea what those words really meant. Eben-ezer translated is, "The stone of help". Samuel raised this Eben-ezer or stone, as a monument to remember what that the Lord had done to deliver Israel from the Philistines.

This painting is my Ebenezer, my monument to the Rock of my Redeemer, my Stone of Help. It illustrates the idea that God often brings His people to struggle in the wilderness. Moses, John the Baptist, and Christ all went to the wilderness as a time of teaching and preparation. I came to understand why Christ is so often called the Stone of Israel in my wilderness experience. He was my sure foundation, the one I held to when all else were gone. He was my refuge. I knew if I held on to Him, I could not fall.

"Rising Up"

The Savior told His disciples repeatedly that He would die and then rise again, but each time they were confused and weren't sure what He meant. After all, who else had been resurrected before?

"And they kept that saying with themselves, questioning one with another what the rising from the dead should mean." -Mark 9:10

Yet, the theme of rising again is prevalent throughout much of Christ's ministry. He said to the man with the withered hand, "Rise up, and stand forth in the midst. And he arose and stood forth" (Luke 6:8). He said to the man at the pool of Bethseda, "Rise, take up thy bed, and walk"(John 5:8). He said to the daughter of Jairus, "arise"(Mark 5:41). It seems there is a pattern of the Savior offering healing, and then commanding the healed to "rise up".

And so, after so many tears, I began to feel Him whisper to me, as He healed my heart, "Daughter, rise up."

"...I say unto thee, arise."

Mark 5:41

"Let Go"

Six months or so after the death of my son, I felt the weight of grief like never before. I cried daily. It seemed like I would have to grieve forever. I let a lie be whispered to me that if I let my grief go, then I never loved. The lie said that the grief was all I had left of my son and to let it go was to let him go. So I carried it around with me, much like this black balloon

Then one day I was studying the Old Testament and found that during the Law of Moses there were a couple different sacrifices that required two animals: one that would be slain and one that would be let go. I saw a beautiful symbolism, that once an atonement had been made, then we should also let go.

I went to God in prayer, I was really honest with Him. I spoke with Him like I would speak to my dad. I put all my grief on the table and over time that weight was lifted. Like the sins that were laid upon the scapegoat in the Old Testament, I laid my grief upon the Savior and through His atonement He took it away. What was so beautiful was that I then learned a truth that it wasn't the grief that held me to my son, it was my love for him that did, and once I let go, that love was intensified, not diminished.

"The sacrifices of God are a broken spirit: a broken an

contrite heart..."
Psalm 51:17

"The Release"

Designing this composition was a struggle because I wanted to include the beautiful face of the model, but I realized that the hands said all that I needed to say. I love how they are pointing upward but also turned outward. For it is only through God's grace, made possible through the atonement of His Son, Jesus Christ, that we are able to let go and find peace. And it is only by keeping our hands facing outward that we are able to find joy again through service. I also realized that it's only when we release the balloon, that our hands are free to use them to do what God intends us to do.

"...Our God whom we serve is able to deliver us..."

Daniel 3:17

"Reach"

The Savior commanded Thomas, "Reach hither thy finger, and behold my hands; and reach hither thy hand, and thrust it into my side: and be not faithless, but believing." (John 20:27) I love the verb *reach* in this phrase because it brings with it the feeling of stretching, of action. He didn't tell Thomas to just touch his hand, He asked him to reach, the verb itself connoting a form of faith.

I know it will probably be a while before any of us will be able to obtain a physical witness of the Savior, but I think the command to "reach" and to "be not faithless, but believing," applies to all of us today. I know that as I reach for Him, as I strive to find and follow Him, His Spirit speaks to mine, and I obtain a witness that He lives, and perhaps in an even more powerful way than Thomas did.

"Reach hither thy finger, and behold m
hand, and thrust it into my side: and b

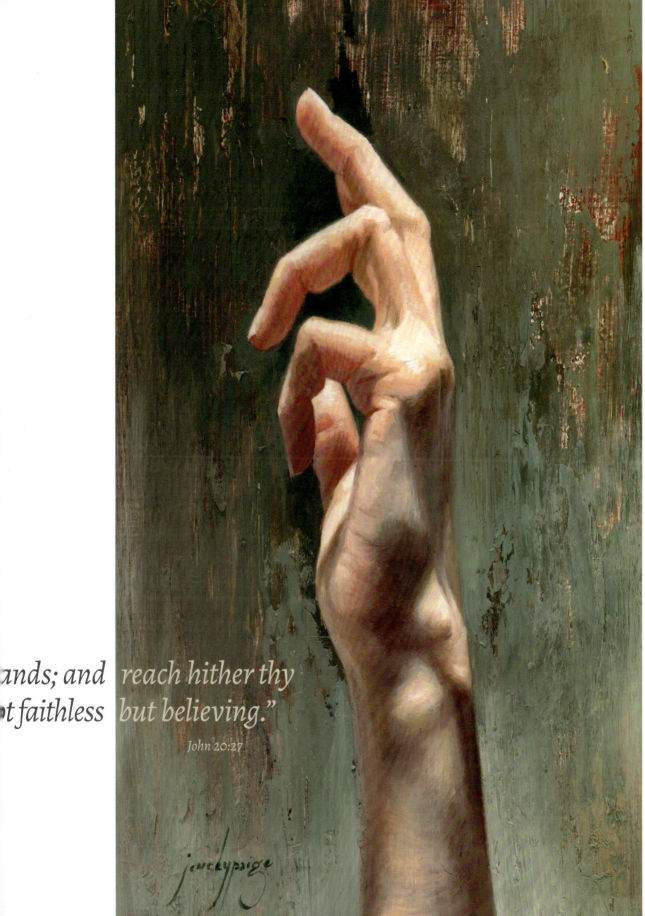

...ands; and reach hither thy ...t faithless but believing."

John 20:27

"Therefo
Go

"Waiting for Answers"

I had so many questions. I knew the direction God wanted me to go, but was tripping up on the details. Every day it felt like this, and my neck was starting to hurt. We live in a world of instant gratification when it comes to obtaining information, most answers are only an internet search away, but when the answers we really need can only come from Heaven, it can be hard to wait. The beautiful thing is, however, as I worked on this painting, the solutions I was looking for came. I know that God hears and answers our prayers. We might have to wait a day, weeks, months, or even years, but as we look, the answers will come.

will look unto the Lord; I will wait for the
my salvation: my God will hear me."

Micah 7:7

"The Student"

When it comes to becoming a great painter, I've learned that technical skill is only a small part of the process. The real struggle comes in training your eyes to see. If you can't see accurately, then you'll never paint accurately no matter how advanced the skill.

In both art and in spiritual matters, I've been trying to expand my sight. I've been trying to listen to my teachers more intently. I have so much yet to learn. Many times during the Savior's ministry, He healed the blind. And in many ways, we come here to earth blinded by the veil and it is only through Him that we will ever see clearly again.

"For now we see through a glass darkly; but the
I know in part; but then shall I known even

"Or what shall a m

"Holding Back"

As our personal relationship with God progresses, we might come to road blocks in the way. In order to keep going, the obstacle must be removed. This causes a type of continual sacrifice. We give up our grudges, our judgments, our fears, social media, and our favorite TV show: anything that is keeping us from Him. The problem is, sometimes we really like that road block or we feel very justified in it and it can be hard to let go of. But then the question is, "Yes, but do you love it more than God?"

e in exchange for his soul?"

(Mark 8:37)

"When Upside Down is Right Side Up"

The word "turn" connotes not only a change of position, but also an evolution into something else. When I paint, I often turn or rotate my paintings while I'm working on them. This means I often find myself painting portraits upside down. I do this because each rotation offers a different perspective, and I can see more clearly adjustments that need to be made. Therefore, as I turn my painting, I'm also turning it one layer at a time into the masterpiece I hope for. I believe God may do the same thing to us. Just when we feel like we have a handle on life, He'll turn things upside down. This can be terrifying at first, but each change offers us new sight and opportunities to learn and grow. Each change can bring refinement from the Master.

"Turn thou us unto thee, O Lord, and we shall be turne

"Therefore we a[re buried with him by baptism into death: that like] as Christ w[as raised up from the dead by the glory of the] Father, eve[n so we also should walk in newness of life.]"

"Renewal"

No matter how dark the night, there is always the hope of the dawn. I love that there is always a new day on the horizon. Each night is like a death, a sleep, and each morning we rise again. We sacrifice our broken hearts and allow Christ to give us a new one. We let go of the old, and trust that Christ can make new. Christ's power over death promises a physical resurrection, but also a new life to those left behind in death's wake.

uried with him by baptism into death: that like
ised up from the dead by the glory of the
we also should walk in newness of life"

Romans 6:4

"Daily Drink"

Recovering from a great loss isn't something that happens in one moment, it is a slow, deliberate process. It's something that must be worked at every day. In order to obtain new life, we must drink from the Living Waters daily. The greatest tool I found for healing was reading the word of God, writing in a journal, and praying every day. This daily devotional practice allowed His healing waters to flow into my life and hope to shine on the horizon.

"But whosoever drinketh of the water that I shall give him shall never thirst; but the water that I shall give him shall be in him a well of water springing up into everlasting life."

John 4:14

"Grace in the Fall"

I see the turning of the seasons as a beautiful symbol of renewal. The earth dies and comes alive again every year. Fall is my favorite season and isn't it interesting that the colors and beauty of the world become so intense right before everything seems to die? If you had never known spring before, you might think that all was lost. Yet, the snow will melt and new life will rise. Even so, Christ's grace makes it possible for our personal winters to turn into spring. He can brace us in our falls, in those unexpected changes of life. He can catch us in our falls, when we are prey to human weakness. His atonement covers for the entire fall of man. When I look at this painting, I also think of the courage of mother Eve in her fall, the trust she had in the Savior's promises. I will look to Christ in every fall, and remember that spring will come, joy will follow sorrow.

me boldly unto the throne of grace, that we may
find grace to help in time of need."

Hebrews 4:16

"Unveiling"

When we're right in the middle of a struggle, a kind of veil is placed over our eyes. We can't see or understand what God is doing with us, or why we would have to experience the deep trenches of a particular trial. All we can feel is pain and all we know is sorrow. Like the snow of winter, it's uncomfortable and bleak. However, as we choose to trust, and continue to turn towards Christ, over time that veil of darkness is lifted. As we look back, we can begin to see wisdom and beauty. As we look back, we can see God's hand moving in our lives. I believe as Paul instructed, that as we turn our hearts to Christ, the veil is taken off a piece at a time.

"But their minds were blinded: for until this da untaken away...; which veil is done awa

"maineth the same veil
Christ."
Corinthians 3:14

"Coming Full Circle"

This painting was ugly for a long time. However, I kept painting because I have learned from experience that the difference between an ugly painting and a beautiful one is just time and hard work. I had turned so many rough starts into lovely finishes that I was confident this one would follow the same pattern.

Similarly, in life we sometimes go through ugly experiences. There are times that we'll want to give up on the whole thing all together. However, if we trust the Master Artist at work, if we have confidence in His abilities, we will find that He can turn the most horrific of experiences into ones that purify and beautify our souls.

In the end we can look back and see His handiwork. The obstacles will be cleared, the questions will find answers, the problems solved, and circumstances will be understood. In that moment everything comes full circle and our hearts swell with gratitude. In that moment of joy and thanks, our hearts connect with Heaven, and we recognize His mercies. Look for circles in life and you will find them."

rk together for good to them that love God"

Romans 8:28

"The Invitation"

I continue to be amazed at how much Jesus Christ wants us to have a relationship with Him. He doesn't just want us to know about Him, He wants us to know Him personally. I tried most my life to learn about Him, but it wasn't until my heart was broken that I really came to know who He was. It was in the trenches, in the darkest of nights, that this extended hand meant the most. There were days I questioned Him, the damage was too great, could He really bring the pieces back together? Now, I can honestly say, "Yes". He is the healer He always promised to be. He was my rock in the wilderness, my hope for healing. He was the means by which I could give up grief and discover a greater love. He is my teacher, the one encouraging me forward, expanding my sights. He is my hope and my promise that I will see my son again someday

"Then spake Jesus again unto them, saying, I am the lig
he that followeth me shall not walk in darkness, b

"...the world: ...all have the light of life."

John 8:12

Art and text © 2019 Jenedy Paige
For more information about Jenedy Paige and her art
visit www.jenedypaige.com

Visit www.havenlight.com to discover more inspirational art products featuring
Jenedy Paige and other award winning artists.

All rights reserved.
No part of this book may be reproduced, altered, trimmed, laminated, mounted or
combined with any text or image to produce any form of derivative work.

Nor may any part of this book be transmitted in any form or by any means, electronic or mechanical,
including photographing and recording, or by any information storage and retrieval system,
without permission in writing from the publisher.

ISBN: 978-1-733-9066-0-9

Published by HavenLight
American Fork, UT 84003
www.HavenLight.com